From Broken Pieces to Peace

KIMI Y BIVINS

ISBN 978-1-951490-61-4 (Print)
ISBN 978-1-951490-62-1 (Digital)

Copyright © 2017 by Kimi Y Bivins
All rights reserved. No part of this publication may be reproduced, distributed, or transmitted in any form or by any means, including photocopying, recording, or other electronic or mechanical methods without the prior written permission of the publisher.

Photography by Michael Moorer: Facebook.com/michaelmoorerphotography

Printed in the United States of America

Contents

To My Beautiful Angel 5
To the Son I Never Had 7
Introduction 9

Chapter 1	Overcome by the Blood of the Lamb and the Word of My Testimony 11
Chapter 2	Boundaries between You and the Opposite Sex 14
Chapter 3	Sensible Boundaries for Family, Friends, and Church Family 19
Chapter 4	If I've Heard One, I've Heard Them All—Church Clichés 21
Chapter 5	The Old Trusty Checklist 24
Chapter 6	When a Man Finds a Wife 35
Chapter 7	For My Kings—The Missing Sons of God 44
Chapter 8	My Sisters, My Queens, and Princesses You Are More Than the Beautiful Skin You're In 47

Chapter 9	Poetic Heartfelt Moments	56
Chapter 10	Getting out of Relationship Ruts and Staying out	86
Chapter 11	Advice from My Dear Mom and Grandmother	103
Chapter 12	You Are Not Broken: My Conclusion	105

To My Beautiful Angel

You are the beautiful child I've always dreamed of. You are the one I've longed to protect. I prayed you would surpass me and you have. With no regrets, I've enjoyed the very moment you came into my life and everyday thereafter. But I do wish I could've shown you what true love between a man and woman or husband and wife looked like. I do wish you had that strong father figure in your life I even desired myself. That wonderful man called your father to bring all men up against to know the difference between genuine love and those not genuine at all. But I believe from this day forward, you will find that true love. You've experienced enough heart breaks of your own at such a young age. Not from the absence of teachings from your loving mother.

I've always wanted to shield you from the pain of unnecessary rejection due to the lack of sensitivity from a few unlearned men nowadays. I could only give you what I knew. And I pray in the future it was enough, my sweet Angel. Thankfully with much prayer and our close relationship with the Father from above . . . all is well. Do me a favor, my sweet heart, never stray away from what you've learned.

Pass it down to your children. It is our legacy.

Love you my li'l beauty,
Mom

To the Son I Never Had

Often I wondered what you would've been like. Surely you would've been a well-mannered young man. You would've been tuned in to your sensitive side. That's all I could do. I could've been tough but not tough enough. I'm not your father and would never be able to take his place nor would I try to. You would have complete respect for women. Disrespect would be far from your intellect because you wouldn't be able to fathom someone mistreating your mother, sister, future daughter or any woman close to you. Only a protector with all your might. You'd know how to provide for your household. Being responsible would be the only option. I could only imagine how closely you would watch me. How much you would've loved. I'd pray you'd be a praying young man. Your priorities would be in order. You would be the all-around young respectful young man I'd hope and dream of. You'd be such a joy to raise. I could only imagine.

    Love you the son I could only have imagined,
                                                  Mom

Introduction

My passion is being used by the Father to aid in healing and restoration of broken hearts. On the road to a strong recovery from a shattered heart myself, I found this very thing—my healing. I've learned even more to trust the Father and his plan. No longer will I question him by saying, "Why me" but "How can I assist you to assist others?" I pray after reading this book, you will find exactly what you're looking for or close to your healing experience. I desire this book to be something you can and will enjoy but can apply it to your life. I'm sure like me, you've read many books on how to find the love of your life. But I desire you find your final road to complete healing from past baggage first before you meet that true love of your life. Let's take this journey together by putting the pieces back together. Moving you "From Broken Pieces to Peace."

Chapter 1

Overcome by the Blood of the Lamb and the Word of My Testimony

Allow me to share my testimony as a believer in Christ that happens to be single at the age of forty-five (and will be single on August 27, 2016).

My mother was seventeen and pregnant by a married man. She dated him before he was, but it ended. Why she went back, I have no idea. But I was the product of dysfunction. Satan had a plan, but little did he know the Father had one too!

Fast forward after having me in Newark, NJ, she returned home to Alabama a few weeks later. Months later she started dating her first husband and married him after I turned a year old.

Over the years as a child and a young teenager I didn't get the opportunity to spend a lot of time with my biological father. Honestly, looking back at my younger years, it was a little dysfunctional. There was always a tug of war in my soul between my mom, my siblings (my mom's kids) and Dad who raised me, and my biological father with his children to include several other outside children. My loyalty should've never been split, but it was.

I can't remember either man giving me what I needed through word or deed as a daughter. I never felt beautiful or secure as a young woman.

I don't ever recall being the one in school that young boys had eyes for. At least it was not expressed to me. In school I had no special flowers being sent to me for Valentine's Day. I was never that special one in the eyes of anyone. Yet I was raped at the age of twenty by someone I was fond of. I was almost abducted at the age of nineteen from a bus station. Back then there were no cell phones. Seems scary, huh? It was.

I ended up in an inappropriate relationship with a married man at the age of eighteen and had to watch him being beaten because he was so drunk that he shoved me out of a moving car while they watched. I could go on and on about the inappropriate relationships I've been in.

But the one place I felt I could find true stability was the church. I truly believed by accepting Jesus Christ as my Lord and savior in February 1995 I would finally find peace. Boy, was I completely wrong. There are just as many, if not more, predators in the church. I could not believe it. It seems as though many have decided after going to the clubs at night made a bee line for the church on Sunday mornings. Church used to be the place you would be able to find a good wholesome spouse. I wonder if that ship sailed long ago and every now and then comes in and drop off a great catch. From the pulpit to the door, you had better question motives nowadays. I've experienced more heart break after giving my life to Christ. Yes, most want to contribute your failed relationships to your upbringing, the relationship you had with your parents. Remember we are supposed to be speaking of believers/followers of Christ. From my own personal experiences, I can see now the game plan has definitely changed. Remember snakes were in the Garden of Eden too. And the last I checked, poisonous or not . . . they all bite.

Chapter 2

Boundaries between You and the Opposite Sex

Get wisdom, get understanding: forget it not; neither decline from the words of my mouth.

—Proverbs 4:5

After many failures in the relationship department I figured it was time to examine my heart and learn from my mistakes. Yes, I make mistakes *but* in these days and time where commitment is at an all-time low, it is high time I protect my heart and put boundaries in place to protect my interests. It is so true of the old saying, "You can't expect different results by doing the same thing. To get different results, you have to do something you've never done before." It's time for a change.

Well, let's see. Here are some of my strong suggestions:

Only meet in public—never meet at each other's home, I would dare say, in the first ninety days. As impatient as people are nowadays, if the individual's heart is not in the right place, it (the relationship) won't last a month.

Don't accept just texts from anyone. If they can't take out the time to call you, then don't allow them to waste a lot of as matter of fact any of your time.

This one is huge for me . . . I wouldn't dare accept a date from anyone through social media especially Facebook. I've heard of success stories through dating sites, but Facebook in my opinion shouldn't be considered a dating site. It's only for stalkers, predators, and cheap thrills. I'm sure there are a few success stories from Facebook. But this shouldn't be your sole purpose.

Preferably if you are dating in public, there shouldn't be any kissing and hugging. There should be absolutely no sex. Sex should be saved for marriage. If the other person is suggesting sex, this is more than likely all they want or expect from you and nothing more. I'm speaking from experience. There are more bad apples out there than good.

Get your own woman/man. Don't date someone else's spouse, boyfriend/girlfriend, boo thing or booty call. If they say that are kind of seeing someone and there's nothing serious between them, it is. More than likely you should not investigate to see. If the person is divorced or just broke up with their significant other, give them at least six months to a year before even considering them as a partner. You do not want to be someone's rebound. If you're the rebound, more than likely you will always be on the short end of the stick. Those individuals are simply not over the other person and more than likely still emotionally attached to them. And your feelings *will not* be considered. Just know during that period after the initial breakup, they *will* be emotionally unavailable and will only use you for a *temporary void filler*. If you are fortunate enough to land a ring out of the deal, woman, you may still be settling. I don't desire to be with someone if their whole heart is not with me. And many times, this is the case. Don't kid yourself or be too cocky about it. I'm not meaning to come off as negative. The facts most of the time are facts. Especially if you allow your emotions to be involved through sexual contact.

Remember, you're not supposed to be having sex during the process of looking for or locating your spouse. Please allow yourself to date a few people before allowing your heart to settle on the first one you see. Many times, if sex is involved, your judgment *will be* cloudy. Your heart should be saved for your God ordained spouse. There will be less disappointment if they decide to bail or break it off if there was no sex or physical touching involved.

Treat everyone as a friend not a potential spouse please. Just get this notion out of your head upfront. Don't allow yourself to be caught up with the outer covering/package—once you unwrap it, you may not like the gift inside. Most women, if we are truthful, have walked the man down the aisle in our minds. *But you just met* him five minutes ago. I was that woman I know.

Addressing the ladies: When a man tells you he's not interested in a relationship but doesn't mind having sex . . . don't be a fool and say, "That's okay, I'm not interested in a relationship either." *You are lying through your teeth* We are not built that way. We are nurturers by trade. We give love easily spiritually and unfortunately with our bodies. Truthfully you desire a relationship, even marriage. Why lie? If you ask the hard question upfront, "Are you ready to be married within the first six months to a year?" You'd know exactly who to weed out of your life. Most men at best are not ready. They are looking for a perverted sexual experience. *Not all men*, but there are many. Most men will lean toward the path of least resistance. *Again I said, not all men* are this way. Don't fall for this reverse psychology and end up in bed with someone *who will* break your heart. Don't have regrets you *can* prevent. And after hearing and seeing this advice, if you continue to fall for this . . . there's no one to blame at the moment but *you*. I pray this seed is planted in your spirit, and someone comes along and water it. But the Father will give the increase.

Don't give or loan the people you just met money to pay their bills. They made it up to this point without you, and they will continue to make it without you. Just point them in another direction.

This clouds their/your vision too. You wouldn't know for sure if they care about you or care more about you meeting their needs at the moment. Once you start this habit, they will continue to ask until you stop. Trust, I'm speaking from experience.

Chapter 3

SENSIBLE BOUNDARIES FOR FAMILY, FRIENDS, AND CHURCH FAMILY

Please make it clear to your family and friends that you are not interested in their matchmaking skills or blind dates. They seem to always make you the subject of all the meetings and the fact that you are not married. Information of course you are privy of . . . duh. Let them know . . . when there's a future date of a wedding, you will inform them of this information. Until then, who, what, when, where, and why is between you and the Lord. Keep them in their place. Don't disrespect them, especially your parents, but be very stern on this issue and *don't* let up. Sooner or later they will get the picture.

Don't let them know when you start dating. It would be in your best interest not to even mention it. Unless it's serious. And remember, you're an adult. It's your business.

When the first negative offense or argument occurs—and it will happen; disagreements do happen—please do not mention it to your family, friends or church members. Usually it's something as simple as they didn't respond back to you in a timely manner you thought was appropriate. Those closest to you have a habit of blowing things way out of proportion. And most times, they have a habit of inserting themselves into your business. They will assume, if you told them once, then they should be a permanent fixture or counselor to you in the near future. Sometimes it's just human nature of busybodies.

Again, keep your business to yourself, those closest to you have a habit of not overlooking any shortcomings in your potential date/partner but want you to overlook every shortcoming in their partner.

Chapter 4

IF I'VE HEARD ONE, I'VE HEARD THEM ALL—CHURCH CLICHÉS

Is it just me or am I the only unmarried person that have heard everything in the book as to why I am not married or what I should be doing while I wait? I seriously doubt it. If you are single, I'm sure you have heard all that will be mentioned! It's the funniest thing to me. I used to be so emotional while hearing the many clichés. It's time to chew up the meat and spit out the bones. And the few clichés I'm about to mention are bones. Trust me! Laugh out loud!

CLICHÉ NUMBER ONE:

Classic from married couples: "Remember, Jesus is your husband." I know it's a cute gesture and all but last I checked, when Jesus comes back isn't he coming back for the whole body of Christ? If he's only married to singles, then all the married couples will not be in the rapture or on their way to hell once they die. May all the married couples who continue to tell singles this without a second thought miss the rapture. Please stop telling singles this please! It's irritating.

Cliché number two:

"Wait on the Lord, honey, he has someone for you." My reply to this: Uhm, do you realize that a thousand years is like a day to the Father! Bless the Lord, oh my soul! More than likely, the individuals telling this . . . did not wait on theirs. They searched, sought after, and as a matter of fact went in for the kill when they met their potential mates. "Maybe he wants you to get yourself together first or he wants you to minister for him by yourself before you get a man" . . . they may say. If it's about us being perfect through Jesus Christ and not by anything we do . . . then guess what . . . you will never be ready if we must wait until we get ourselves together. This sounds like what I used to say before I got saved. I'm not ready to be saved, I should wait until I'm ready. You weren't ready for kids, but you have them. When you get married, it will be a constant experience of learning and loving one another.

Cliché number three:

"Don't sleep with him/her or they will leave you." Well, of course, this is true that we should not, but sir/ma'am, did you wait? I'll wait while you answer that. And more times than not, they will tell you no, they did not wait. Really? Doesn't that frustrate you to no end? And most of the time it is always the married couples that can enjoy sex when they get ready. But thankfully I've chosen to once again vow to purity. These last few headaches-two legged afflictions did it for me. So, I'll definitely wait until mine come for me and walk me down the aisle or take me to the justice of the peace! Ha! And I'm finally okay with waiting!

People have their own free will. I've always wondered about this one. So, certain individuals can do whatever they desire to do. And what they are saying is *you* don't have your own free will. Uhm . . . this may be another book in the making. Just saying.

Know your worth. If the Bible is true and I'm trying not to be deep, I know I'm the head and not the tail. Above only and never beneath. I've heard it all my saved life. I've read it in black and white. I know who I am. This leads me to my next cliché. And the newest one.

"Keep yourself off of the clearance rack or in the vault where the expensive diamonds are." This is a very good saying . . . true it is. *I know who I am.* Are these people speaking to the ones that's about to lose a great thing that will surely bring them favor? I would say not. This is the very reason for many twisted relationships. The ones you should be talking to . . . you don't. Unless it's your child or family member, the ones you shouldn't be talking to . . . you do. So much human carnal judgment and not enough righteous spiritual judgment.

Chapter 5

THE OLD TRUSTY CHECKLIST

After the recent awakening events . . . and *yes*, they were very awakening events. The first thing I did shortly after giving my life to Christ, I heard about the checklist. "What checklist?" You might ask. When I first received salvation, I was told I should have a checklist. And of course, I had my own, with careful prayer. After five years or so after writing my list, it was trashed or either compromised. But now as I said, after the awakening or enlightening last events, I see why the Holy Spirit gave me the certain things on my list to adhere by.

But before writing a list, you must find out who you are as a person. *Do* you know who you are? What are your likes and dislikes? What are your limits? Have you worked on you? If not, I suggest you do that. If not there will be much compromise that will bring you much pain. Knowing who you are is half the battle.

Now I will discuss certain things you may consider putting on your list.

Do you want a spouse that's ever been married? I can be scripturally deep on this answer, but I won't. Personally, I've decided that I don't desire anyone that's ever been married. I want to be the first and only. My mother is remarried, and I have listened to her many times refer to her last spouse. I believe there will always be a comparison between the first and current spouse. I've never been married before so the first will be my last. It's just my opinion, but that will be an irritant for me.

Do you want a spouse that has children or want children? Let's just put it this way, I am almost passed child bearing age. I have one child. She will be twenty-four in December. I don't desire to start all over again with more children. Now will I want a spouse with children? This is still in the air with me. Am I willing to trust a man with children and the mother is still in the picture? Will my spouse include me in all the plans with this child? And to be with me? *I will* be in every plan concerning that child with *no exceptions*. It's not that I don't trust him, but I definitely *will not* trust her. Fortunately, with me, which is a rarity, I don't communicate much with my daughter's father. He's in a relationship, and furthermore he's able to communicate with my daughter without me. And trust, I am completely happy about that. If I decide to be with a man with children . . . they may have to have adult children supporting themselves. And needing him only when necessary.

Do you want a spouse with or without an education or degree? I current have a degree and am working on another one. Do you want someone that's constantly trying to improve themselves or are you wanting someone that's constantly always making excuses as to why they haven't started yet? But of course there are many resources on the internet. Nowadays most millionaires are college dropouts *but* they did *attempt* college. So if you have a degree, more than likely you may want to be with someone obtaining or have obtained a degree.

Do you want a spouse with a job and benefits or with an entrepreneurial spirit? More than likely you should be with someone that has a job for sure. If they are an entrepreneur, they need to be well established for some years and not in the beginning stages. At my age, I do not have time or am making the time for someone that's not financially stable. *Period*. I have a job with benefits, and they will definitely have that. I strongly suggest you expect the same.

Will you accept a spouse with bad credit or a lot of debt? Honestly this is a question that need to be asked upfront. If you are an individual with good or great credit, you will not want to marry someone with bad credit. When getting ready to purchase a house or any line of credit, your potential spouse's credit will be considered. Being with someone with bad credit is like throwing money down the drain. You'll be considered for all high interest rate loans.

They definitely have to be in the process of coming back or getting rid of destructive spending habits. Yes, we've all had our credit issues due to the loss of a job, divorce, or other unfortunate events. But there's a difference between coming back from less fortunate events and having bad spending habits. This will lead to my next question.

Do you desire a spouse with a bank account? Honestly and with good common sense, especially if you are older and well established with a bank account, you may want someone with *at least* an emergency fund. They may not know all the ins and outs of investments and have a portfolio but should have an emergency fund. That would be for starters. You don't want to be with someone that only wants you for what you have. You want them to want you for you.

Do you want someone with common sense? It's not enough they have a college degree. There are those who are very intelligent but ask them to do a simple task as boiling water they may not be able to tell you. This is a given, but it leads me to my next question.

Do you want a spouse that knows how to cook? I'm sure this will be big for the fellas. If you are a man that love to eat, you may want to look past a woman's looks. She may be a vegetarian, and you are a steak and potato man. And women, you may want a man that know how to cook as well. You and your spouse can take turns and or enjoy cooking together. As the old saying goes, ladies, the way to a man's heart is his stomach. You may want to learn how to boil more than eggs for your man. Just saying. Glad my mom and grandmother taught me a few things in the kitchen.

Can you accept a spouse with a criminal past? Please be led by the Spirit on this one. Yes, people can change. But whatever their criminal past is . . . it *must be* a part of their *past*. And for me, it definitely depends on what it was, and you may want to request a background check on your own. I would not take their word for me. This is a serious one for me. Sometimes a leopard never loses their spots, as my grandmother use to say.

Do you want a spouse with different spiritual beliefs than yours or not saved at all? I do not desire to be with anyone that believes in anything other than Jesus Christ. They must've given their life to Christ. I'm not saying they must be perfect. I do understand that no one is. This is one thing I refuse to compromise on, period. There are many who say they believe in him, but they don't. Trust if they don't, you will know it. Watch how they treat you. If they ask you to compromise on your beliefs . . . this is a red flag. Many times different religious beliefs will clash and definitely a person that does not confess salvation at all.

Do you desire a mate of the same or different culture or race? You may not be able to help who you fall for. Some limit themselves in this area. Uhm, I have decided to take all limits off as long as they treat me with respect and dignity. Put my needs at number one.

Do desire someone with a good sense of humor? I love to laugh and laugh a lot. Having a good sense of humor is important to me. When I'm having a bad day can you make me laugh or are you a miserable complainer? Can you laugh at yourself and not be so serious about everything? Life is too short and can pass you by pretty quick if you don't watch it.

Do you want someone that is known for a compromised integrity? Most people don't want a known liar, cheater, or thief. I don't think this is the issue. The issue is . . . most people think they are good enough to talk these people into changing. Most are who they are and will not change unless *they* desire to change. *You* will *not* be able to change them. Your love will not change them. And again as the old saying goes, "Change ain't change until it's been changed."

Does it matter if your spouse is a giver or very stingy? If you are a giver, you would want a giver but someone that can maintain a sense of control over their spending. There is a difference between a giver and a spender. Spenders have a habit of allowing more going out than coming in. Givers love to give but don't mind investing in something with a sure return.

Once you're married, what you will want or expect sexually from your spouse? This is tricky but should come within the first few months of dating. This must be a deep conversation. Do you like certain sexual acts or no? Having multiple partners should be off the table, period. If they desire this now . . . you had better run. You *will never* be able to satisfy them. Are they sex addicts? Are they bisexual? Do they like sex at all? *Do* they have health problems that will prevent them from having sex? You better ask as many questions as needed. And there is no need in being shy! You are a grown man/woman. You had better ask. You know for sure what you will and will not deal with.

Do you have plans of getting married in the near future? By not having sex right away, you may have this answer right away too. Tell them you desire to be married in the near future. If they are not ready to be married in the near future, this tells you two things: they are truly not ready, and you would be wasting your time or you are *not* the *one* for them, and you will still be wasting your time. This will weed out everyone necessary upfront. And it shields your heart from unnecessary pain and foolishness plus foolish people.

Do you want your spouse to be younger or older than you? My personal preference is to be with someone that's not young enough to be my child nor old enough to be my father. This is definitely a personal preference you must decide. For us women I've always heard the saying, "It's better to be an old man's honey than a young man's fool." It's just my preference also, but I desire a man that's older.

Do you desire a mate with health issues? This was a big one for my grandmother. She used to always tell us to check out the *whole* family. Families have hereditary diseases. If you are desiring children with your mate, you may want to know by asking the upfront questions. Also, do they have HIV or other issues? Please ask.

Does outer appearance matter to you? Of course, love is what we're looking for, but if we're all honest, we are led at times by our eyes. Me being a woman, I will consider height. I am only 5'1 and some change. And I do *not* desire someone shorter than I. Not even close. I desire someone that tries to keep himself in shape. I'm not an exercise buff, but I do care about what or how I look in my clothing. Being a retired military vet after twenty-six years, neatness still matters.

Do you desire to be with a mate you don't have chemistry with? Chemistry can be a factor also. Some people are naturally attracted to people upfront. I've been around someone I've had a natural attraction to for years, but issues were always in the way to act upon it. Chemistry is an important thing for me. If you just don't feel it then definitely don't force it. There are some things that just feel right and some not.

Do you desire a spouse that's family oriented? I can tell you this . . . from what I've witnessed it will make for a better marriage. I understand that you may say, "I will not be married to his/her family." Oh, but you will. I desire it all, and it's not impossible. As I've stated before, I'm not exactly a spring chicken. So, my patience may be challenged. Not sure I desire to be in a family full of drama. But if you believe you are with the right one in spite of their family, just make sure they are all about you. You must come first. This will lead me to my next question.

Do you desire to be with a spouse that doesn't honor or respect their parents? No matter the underlying issues, parents should always be honored just for the fact they loved you enough to birth you. More than likely if your spouse does not honor and respect their parents, they will not honor or respect you. Anger and abuse issues could appear in your relationship sooner rather than later.

Do you desire to be with a spouse that's high maintenance? This may be a question for the men, but then again, there are men who stay in the mirror as much as we do. I love to keep myself up, but as I've stated, I'm a twenty-six-year retired vet. Let's just say training for war all those years, makeup nor hair was on the brain or a first priority. Waking up early enough to get dressed and promptly starting my day is important to me. If your lady is grabbing her makeup case on the way out of a burning building, she may be high maintenance (chuckles to myself).

Do you desire a mate that challenges your pet peeves? I am prompt. I don't deal well with lateness. When they're eating, do they drag their fork against their teeth? Can you deal with snoring? Can you deal with belching and release of gas (I'm trying to be nice)?

Do you desire a procrastinator or a go getter for a spouse? Personally procrastination for me would be a relationship killer. This is more than likely why many relationships *never* get off the ground. The reason why many miss the relationship of a lifetime thinking they can always find something better and unfortunately end up with something worse. And possibly end up going back to bondage you left.

Your Trusty Checklist

Use the area below to write your own checklist or note based on what you read.

_____
_____
_____
_____
_____
_____
_____
_____
_____
_____
_____
_____
_____
_____
_____
_____
_____
_____
_____
_____

KIMI Y BIVINS

Chapter 6

When a Man Finds a Wife

Whoso findeth a wife findeth a good thing,
and obtaineth favour of the Lord

—Proverbs 18:22, KJV

This is everyone's favorite scripture to use. Let the man find you is what I was always told. And this might've been true in the twentieth century. Let me give you Kimi's take on this. Look at the society we live in today. Social media is at an all-time high. Reality TV seems to govern the reality of dating and what to look for in a mate. Everything has a sexual overtone to it. Sexual perversion is at an all-time high. Extra silicone breasts and women's backsides spread are in even if pads are added. Half-dressed women seem to be better. You no longer have to go to the clubs, the clubs have moved to the churches. So called saved men are going for the unsaved women just because they say they are holding out on sex until married. In case you didn't realize it, men . . . the women are still unsaved. Texting has taken over and less face to face communication is the new style of communicating. Now keeping your relationship, a secret is the new *in* thing to do.

And believe me, I am an old fashion type of lady. I love to see men still taking women out on dates, surprising her with flowers, etc. Wanting me to be known as someone's lady is still important.

In this chapter I am speaking to the people who say they are believers in Jesus/Yeshua, those who still believe in the Bible and its power. Most nowadays treat it as a binder with pages. It's just another book on a shelf. Let's see what the Father intended from the beginning before the fall in the garden:

> [21]And the Lord God caused a deep sleep to fall upon Adam, and he slept: and he took one of his ribs, and closed up the flesh instead thereof; [22]And the rib, which the Lord God had taken from man, made he a woman, and brought her unto the man. [23]And Adam said, This is now bone of my bones, and flesh of my flesh: she shall be called Woman, because she was taken out of Man. [24]Therefore shall

> a man leave his father and his mother, and shall cleave unto his wife: and they shall be one flesh. ²⁵And they were both naked, the man and his wife, and were not ashamed. (Genesis 2:21–24 KJV)

Hhhhhhmmmm . . . regardless of what we think, Father never intended on anyone chasing after anyone. Of course, for years I heard the foolishness that men are hunters. They like to hunt their women. In case you've missed it. Women are not animals. To me this perception has led men to treating women as animals/prey.

"There is a way that seems right to a man, but its end is the way to death," (Proverbs 14:12 ESV).

But *it* is my belief Proverbs 18:22 "When a man finds a wife" is speaking about a wife's character. What is your definition of a wife? According to Merriam-Webster: a married woman: the woman someone is married to. As you can see, this seems very vague coming from people. Hhhhhmmmm . . . let's possibly find a more in depth definition . . . you guessed it.

> The words of king Lemuel, the prophecy that his mother taught him. ²What, my son? and what, the son of my womb? and what, the son of my vows? ³Give not thy strength unto women, nor thy ways to that which destroyeth

kings. ⁴It is not for kings, O Lemuel, it is not for kings to drink wine; nor for princes strong drink: ⁵Lest they drink, and forget the law, and pervert the judgment of any of the afflicted. ⁶Give strong drink unto him that is ready to perish, and wine unto those that be of heavy hearts. ⁷Let him drink, and forget his poverty, and remember his misery no more. ⁸Open thy mouth for the dumb in the cause of all such as are appointed to destruction. ⁹Open thy mouth, judge righteously, and plead the cause of the poor and needy. *¹⁰Who can find a virtuous woman? for her price is far above rubies. ¹¹The heart of her husband doth safely trust in her, so that he shall have no need of spoil. ¹²She will do him good and not evil all the days of her life. ¹³She seeketh wool, and flax, and worketh willingly with her hands. ¹⁴She is like the merchants' ships; she bringeth her food from afar. ¹⁵She riseth also while it is yet night, and giveth meat to her household, and a portion to her maidens. ¹⁶She considereth a field, and buyeth it: with the fruit of her hands she planteth a vineyard. ¹⁷She girdeth her loins with strength, and strengtheneth her arms. ¹⁸She perceiveth that her merchandise is good: her candle goeth not out by night. ¹⁹She layeth her hands to the spindle, and her hands hold the distaff. ²⁰She stretcheth out her hand to the poor; yea, she reacheth forth her hands to the needy. ²¹She is not afraid of the snow for her household: for all her household are clothed with scarlet. ²²She maketh herself coverings of tapestry; her clothing is silk and purple. ²³Her husband is known in the gates, when he sitteth among the elders of the land. ²⁴She maketh fine linen, and selleth it; and delivereth girdles unto the merchant. ²⁵Strength and honour are her clothing; and she shall rejoice in time to come. ²⁶She openeth her mouth with wisdom; and in her tongue is the law of kindness. ²⁷She looketh well to the ways of her household, and eateth not the bread of idleness. ²⁸Her children arise up, and call her blessed; her husband also, and he praiseth her. ²⁹Many daughters have done virtu-*

> *ously, but thou excellest them all. ³⁰Favour is deceitful, and beauty is vain: but a woman that feareth the Lord, she shall be praised. ³¹Give her of the fruit of her hands; and let her own works praise her in the gates.* (Proverbs 31)

For this scripture, I added italicized to point out certain verses in this chapter. I also included the whole chapter instead of starting at the normal verse 10. Guess where this king received his advice from? Notice verse 1, his mother taught him this verse. I wonder if it's common anymore, mothers teaching their sons to stay away from certain women and they actually listen. The Father always intended for the man to lead, but it seems as though from verse 3 to 9 there may be possible reasons why men's choices may end up being challenged. But verses 10–31 gives you a detailed definition straight from the Word of a wife.

Now back to the scripture "when a man finds a wife." I wonder if anyone has ever read the story of Ruth. You know the story about the woman whose husband died. She decides to go back to Bethlehem with her mother-in-law Naomi after her husband died as well. Naomi agreed with her daughter-in-law to glean in Boaz's field, hoping she'd find favor. She also instructed her to go to the threshing floor and lay at his feet around midnight. Hhhhhmmmm. There are times you may have to switch up your plans, ladies. I would dare believe nowadays Naomi may represent the Holy Spirit or an older seasoned mother. You may be receiving instructions from the wrong source. You are limiting yourselves by one scripture.

See for yourselves . . . don't take my word for it.

"And Ruth the Moabitess said unto Naomi, Let me now go to the field, and glean ears of corn after him in whose sight I shall find grace. And she said unto her, Go, my daughter."

Now what if Naomi instructed her to wait until Boaz found her? Ruth might've missed her blessings of a husband and a food supply for her and Naomi. Listening to some of you she would've missed out on being in the very lineage of Jesus.

Here's another few verses of scripture from Ruth.

> [1] Then Naomi her mother in law said unto her, My daughter, shall I not seek rest for thee, that it may be well with thee? [2] And now is not Boaz of our kindred, with whose maidens thou wast? Behold, he winnoweth barley to night in the threshing floor. [3] Wash thyself therefore, and anoint thee, and put thy raiment upon thee, and get thee down to the floor: but make not thyself known unto the man, until he shall have done eating and drinking. [4] And it shall

be, when he lieth down, that thou shalt mark the place where he shall lie, and thou shalt go in, and uncover his feet, and lay thee down; and he will tell thee what thou shalt do. ⁵And she said unto her, All that thou sayest unto me I will do. ⁶And she went down unto the floor, and did according to all that her mother in law bade her. ⁷And when Boaz had eaten and drunk, and his heart was merry, he went to lie down at the end of the heap of corn: and she came softly, and uncovered his feet, and laid her down. ⁸And it came to pass at midnight, that the man was afraid, and turned himself: and, behold, a woman lay at his feet. ⁹And he said, Who art thou? And she answered, I am Ruth thine handmaid: spread therefore thy skirt over thine handmaid; for thou art a near kinsman. ¹⁰And he said, Blessed be thou of the Lord, my daughter: for thou hast shewed more kindness in the latter end than at the beginning, inasmuch as thou followedst not young men, whether poor or rich. ¹¹And now,

> my daughter, fear not; I will do to
> thee all that thou requirest: for all
> the city of my people doth know
> that thou art a virtuous woman.
> (Ruth 3:1–11 KJV)

From the very verse I read, Boaz actually thought she was a virtuous woman even coming at midnight. And notice she anointed herself before going. There was no sex involved. Had we even thought of this . . . "Oh, no! Don't do that! You know what happens at that time of night." At times your own brothers and sisters in Christ are your *worst* enemy. Nowadays this would be considered playing it safe. Please stop giving out negative advice. And anything said without counsel from the Holy Spirit first . . . is a negative in my book. Trust me, I've taken a lot of premature advice. What you may feel in the eyes of the Father to be wrong is right, and what's right in your eyes is totally wrong to him. I am so glad Naomi never discouraged Ruth or used the same tired out cliché lines people use nowadays. I am very sure and more than likely these two women saw the *whole* big picture.

In your spare time, I encourage any woman to read the story of Ruth. There are only four chapters in the book. I pray when you do, the Holy Spirit shows you a totally different perspective.

Chapter 7

For My Kings—
The Missing Sons of God

For the anxious longing of the creation waits eagerly for the revealing of the sons of God.

—Romans 8:19

I long to see the day when the true men of God will just show us women true strength once again. You were created in the very image of the Father. Yes, I understand you've had many shortcomings. But until the man/kings take their rightful place once again, many things on this earth will continue to be in chaos. In the biblical days, blessings always came through the sons' fathers. Where are our strong, handsome men? Excuses can no longer keep you in bondage. Isn't it still true? Who the Son sets free, he is free indeed. Or do you desire to be set free? Will you be the one breaking generational curses in your time? Or will you continue the cycle of defeat? Will you find that one and only and be faithful to her? Will you raise your children to know you as an honorable man, or will they later on know you as a man of dishonor and have to be embarrassed by the legacy you leave them. During events your children are having in school, will you show up or no? Will your daughters have to reap because you were good to them but not their mothers or other women? I've been the product of my biological father's shortcomings/absence more than presence of not being there and having to be raised by another man as his own. Thankfully he (the one that raised me) didn't abandon me. But it didn't help my life any in the relational department. I had to force myself to change my thoughts and habits. I had to change how I saw myself because I wasn't told enough how beautiful I was. I am too old to be the damsel in distress. Too old to play the woman scorned. Yet I, being young, chose to sleep with a young man before marriage and became pregnant. He chose to ignore the fact of information concerning my pregnancy once he was privy to it. Will I continue to blame him? The answer is NO. By the grace and mercy of the Father, I have a beautiful daughter who graduated college in December 2016. I raised her by myself without the pull and tug between loyalties of two different men as I. I gave it all I had. She's had her struggles from time to time, but overall,

I'm blessed to have been an example—a woman of strength she needed.

The Father saved me in the nick of time. The men I chose to lay with, I did without her knowledge. I didn't allow my sins to be her sins by bringing men in my house laying up with them in front of her. She never saw me hustle men out of money just to make ends meet. A job, section 8, the Army Reserves, and food stamps was enough until I got on my feet. She never could say those words "Well, you did it." I eliminated all excuses. I never wanted her to fall prey to a man out of his position as a so-called king and really being on assignment of the devil.

Be a man of integrity. Be a man of honor. Be a man of success. Be a proud protégé or even better than your father. Be a mother's blessing and not the source of her heartaches. Be the example of a man your daughter dreams of. Make it harder for your daughter to settle for a man that means her no good. Be the example of a king, a leader your sons dream of becoming. But you must remember there must be a lot of little steps of doing before you can BE.

Will you leave a legacy of blessings for your children or a legacy of curses? I only desire to provoke your thoughts by asking rhetorical questions. The answers you have for these questions in your heart are between you and your maker.

You can and will be the king you desire.

Chapter 8

My Sisters, My Queens, and Princesses You Are More Than the Beautiful Skin You're In

The King's daughter is all glorious within;
Her clothing is interwoven with gold.

I will cause Your name to be remembered
in all generations; Therefore the peoples
will give You thanks forever and ever.

—Psalm 45:13, 17

My beautiful sisters of all colors, shapes, and brilliant intellects, when will we know and be who we are? When will we stop allowing the curse of Eve to overtake us? When will we allow our men to take their rightful place? Do you realize we can choose who we allow to dwell in our precious courts of time and space? Do you realize the Father thought it not robbery to make us equal to our counterparts, the man? Do you realize that *every* dream, *every* person after Eve came through *us*? Every living, breathing, viable candidate for life. I repeat: In order for it/they to live, it/they must come through *us*. We are more powerful than we actually give ourselves credit yet sensitive enough to remain humble enough to love and nurture anything and anyone. The Father favored us with the most powerful organ besides our hearts—a womb. Even Eve was called the mother of all living. You have the power to kill what you allow to live, my beautiful sisters. Such power we must not forget.

Of course, we were the first to speak to the enemy in the garden. Somehow, I equate this to being more spiritual than our counterparts, the man. We also must realize it was the seed of our womb his feet that bruised the head of the enemy. We have the ability to raise giant killers, kings, queens, even great husbands and fathers. After all everyone will come through our womb with no exceptions.

We have the power to spiritually connect to the Father and believe enough to pray our wayward children home. We have the power to encourage our children to be whatever they desire to be. But we have to be careful not to use that same power destroy our sons and daughters. They are the future mothers, fathers, husbands, and wives. What are we speaking into the atmosphere? I'm guilty of speaking death when I should be speaking life. *We are* the most powerful beings on earth and *never* see yourself as any less. If you are of child bearing age and chose to have or not have children, you must decide now you will be the powerful being *you already* are. We must be positive examples for our children, families, and those we are unaware of who may be watching. We must be honest with ourselves. We have always been taken advantage of. Our hearts desire to see the best in anyone. We are nurturers by trade. But I know for myself, I've been my own worst enemy by allowing the same heart that loves so much lead me into places I should've never been. I challenge you to be wise with your love toward our counterparts. The very ones we breed will cause some of the harshest heartbreaks. I cannot stress it enough. *Guard your heart* We must choose to do what is right at all times. We must always be mindful of the situations we allow ourselves to be in. We've been victims of circumstances for too long but for centuries have been treated like the villain instead. Remember the biblical story of the woman that was caught in the very act of adultery? Where was the man? She couldn't create the situation by herself. Thank the Father for Jesus who came to rescue her from a death sentence. Nowadays, the difference between her and us . . . we were stoned, even if it was with words. I know I have. My character was shot for a long time by the very ones who might've been guilty for the same sin. But I shouldn't have placed myself in that position. We cannot continue to make unhealthy choices such as fornicating before marriage, sleeping with someone's husband or whatever the case may be and continue to expect mercy. Remember we are royalty, we come from royalty. And we must carry ourselves as such. No more excuses.

Chapter 9

Poetic Heartfelt Moments

> My heart overflows with a good theme;
> I address my verses to the King; My
> tongue is the pen of a ready writer.
>
> —Psalm 45:1, NASB

In my moments of being alone, writing poetry have always ministered to me. The Holy Spirit is truly my comforter. When I relied on the comforter, there was always a poetic expression left on my heart. I've always been met with compassion and love, a freedom to express myself to the Father and those around me. There's nothing like being healed through gifts given by the heart of the Father himself. I'm so thankful for this gift. I pray these poems minister to you as much as they did to me.

THIS PAIN THAT I FEEL

This pain that I feel
How did you get here
When will it stop
It seems never, I fear.

For a moment
Feels like eternity
Why can't these valleys
Just let me be?

When will I experience
The mountains on high
But staying there
Is a constant fight.

Lord, help me
To hold to your unchanging hand
as the old folk claimed
There's got to be a way out
From experiencing this kind of pain.

KIMI Y BIVINS

There's pressure in my heart
That ceases to go away
I need a miracle
And it can't wait another day.

Fix it, Jesus
Unless in this I die
I'm tired of going
In between lows and highs.

The pain that I feel
Help me to escape
I need relief now
For this Hell needs to pay.

Come on and bring me
Back to that place of victory
It's mine already
Bondage and hurt you will leave me be.

Lord, let your joy come out of nowhere
Let it strengthen me
It's about that time
My help is come. I'm free indeed!

I Know What It's Like

I know what it's like
To be loved by a king
If but for a moment
I reigned supreme.

I know what it's like
To have been with a knight
In shining armor
A warrior at best
A complete charmer.

I know what it's like
To have been with a beautiful soul
If but for a moment
Now my heart is no longer broken
But mended and made whole.

I know what it's like
To have been loved, not rejected
My soul and dignity still intact
It was definitely tested.

I know what it's like
I preferred my name to still be good and chosen
beautiful memories known but unspoken.

Now I know what it's like
To have been favored by a king
But for a beautiful moment
I will look back and won't regret a thing.

Thank you, King.

My Adoration Is for the Most High

My adoration is for the most high
A place where I go
Suspended in the heavens
Is where I best flow.

I don't mind going to meet with you
Where the atmosphere is pure
No distractions
Not even noises can lure.

Help me stay in this place
I need to be with you
The peace I long for
On my knees is where I'm glued.

Let me adore you
Up close is where I need to be
Let me be drawn
Upon your glory let my eyes see.

My adoration is for the most high
I will continually go
A place of worshipping
And knowing you up close.

KIMI Y BIVINS

My Beauty Is Not for Sale

My beauty is not for sale
Nor will it ever be
No amount can be paid
No large or small fee.

It was sold to the highest bidder
To the Father creator himself
It was nailed to the cross
With Jesus Christ death.

My beauty is not for sale
Nor my worth or self esteem
No need to borrow your crown
When He's made me a queen

Skin dipped in His anointing
I prefer to wait for His Praise
He will exalt me in time
Until then I'll continue to keep my head raised.

I'll continue to step high in my beautiful heels
This beauty is taking me somewhere
To my destiny
He's manifesting his will shortly to fulfill

I'm so glad my beauty is not for sale
From in to out it appears
He made me
I'm at peace. He has calmed my fears.

SEX

In the beginning
God created it
It is the best feeling when right
That will ever exist.

Why did you make it
So beautiful and hard to resist
The art of it
Just to think of it

Takes me to a place
Where time stops in space
Don't want it to end
Let the time continue to suspend.

But wait I'm single
I want this to be my mate
Can we get married now?
Don't make me wait.

After all God created it
It's called sex.

But Momma didn't tell me
About all the affects.

When having it at the wrong time
The emotions unwind
It kept me out of control
It's gripped my soul.

After all God created it
How can it be so bad?
It feels better than the best dessert
Your mouth could taste or ever had

Why didn't my father
Give me all the details—the birds and the bees
Now I'm all caught up in my emotions my feelings
I was not taught how to swim in the deep
It can cause you to believe in a
love that's not really there
Does God really care
Now I'm suspended in air.

Now that I'm a grown woman
Can I still blame it on my parents who
didn't teach me when they should have?
One child later it's too late . . . for that.

I never wanted to be a servant to it
But only to God the Father indeed
Even if I had the instructions
I wonder if I would have taken heed.

Did they marry because of love
Or was it only to have sex?

It's so powerful
The effects
Are everlasting
Sometimes crashing.

Is it my emotions
Or is it really love?
After all it's from God
The creator from above.

After all he created it
I want and need a part or all of it
But Help me to keep control of it.

So I don't be destroyed because of it
Again I say after all He created *it*.

It's You and You Alone

It's you and you alone
That makes my heartbeat
I completely melt
When I hear you speak.

If you only knew
What you do to me
You give me thrills
Your every touch is what I need.

Baby, the way you love me is incredible
You keep bringing me back for more and more
I tried to walk away
But the force you bring is too powerful for sure.

There are places you touched me
No one else could fulfill the need
Baby, keep doing what you do
It completes me.

Absolutely no one on this earth
Has ever come close
It caught me by surprise
I don't think you suppose.

FROM BROKEN PIECES TO PEACE

Since you came in my life
I have been completely undone
No more business as usual
I had to change and become.

You fit into my world
More perfect than a hand in a glove
From the moment I saw you
Is there really first-at-sight love?

I want to get this right
Don't want to mess it up
Tell me when I'm wrong
Don't want to do without your touch.

It's you and you alone
The one I crave
Trying to figure out
How to get you to stay.

It's you and you alone
I want you here forever in my life
Can't see it without you.

Stay here with me and make every
night a good night, baby.

Sex Is Incredible

Sex is incredible
When used in the right context
Don't get it twisted
It has lasting effects.

God created it
To be used between two
Married of course
Intimacy is the goal to be pursued.

It's for procreation
This was God's original intent
But never the less Satan
Uses his perversion to always reinvent.

Sex outside of marriage
Was never supposed to be
Sowing to the flesh
Planting wicked seeds

Of disappointment, heartbreaks
There's a lot at stake
Our righteousness, our right standing
With the one and only son.

What about eternity
After we leave from here
Is this short moment of passion worth
All the torment and fear?

You will experience if you
Continue to disobey this is clear
In His word
Fornicators can't inherit.

The kingdom at all
Against His word
We can't continue to fall
God will give the strength

If we ask
With men this is impossible
But Him a simple task.

Sex is incredible
A feeling or act that can't be denied
Only when it's done right
Between a husband and wife.

It's better to marry than to burn
In lust
He said let us reason together
With him this matter you can discuss.

This is your children's inheritance
It can be rich or poor
This can be passed down to them
Do you really adore them?

How can you teach them about sex
When you're not living right?

Many won't agree
Because of your lack of obedience
They will be lying awake and crying at night.

Our children deserve to see
Higher standards of godliness
But all they're seeing
Is pain and emptiness.

Sex is incredible
Lord, help us to return back to your original intent.
It's only beautiful
When it's your consent

We're gonna get this right come hell or high water
Our bodies are yours
Restore and bring us back in order.

FROM BROKEN PIECES TO PEACE

Protect and shield our minds
From perverted thoughts
We will cast them down
To hell they will be tossed.

We love you enough to obey in this area
Just give us your strength
And we will stay near to ya.

You Are Still in Control

You are still in control
There's no way you're not
At the end of the day
You are all that I've got.

Things and people are always changing
Time is drawing near
Things you are rearranging
When I can't trust anyone else.

You are always faithful and true
You always remain constant and near
People always seem to forsake you.

People always seem to think
They are in control
Have you told them yet?
That it's not so.

Everything still goes by a written script
Before the foundations of the world
They are still confused
Can I share this with them, Sir?

FROM BROKEN PIECES TO PEACE

Naw, I won't
What the heck for
This will be fun to watch
While I'm obedient and begin to soar.

You are in control
I've made no mistake about it
Your promises you keep
All will still manifest in time as you see fit.

I trust you, Father
And your hand
Until you manifest my miracles
I'll continue to stand.

I Ran from the Power

I ran from the power
That was in my own self
Didn't realize my own strength
God gave it to me to compel.

Me into a place of intimacy
With Him
A place where nothing else could be felt
There's no more emptiness left inside.

Your love is so powerful
That's why it's easy for me to confide.

In you, Jesus,
I will no longer run from the power within me
It shields me from disappointments and pain
As a matter of fact, the power gives me victory
In this power it helps me to sustain.

FROM BROKEN PIECES TO PEACE

I can't run from it anymore
I gotta see what's in store
I didn't chose this power

It came looking for me
To give me peace serenity.

I won't run from it anymore
It's in my deepest core.

Thank you for it
I'm worthy of it
I ran from the power
But I say no more!

When You Look at Me

When you look at me
You see nothing but beauty
When you look at me
You see a strong successful city.

When you look at me
You see a princess
When you look at me
I am pure at best.

When you look at me
I am pure and unashamed
When you look at me
I am free from my past and the pain.

When you look at me
There is nothing but confidence
When you look at me
I have received my recompense.

When you look at me
I am at peace with myself
When you look at me
I am blessed beyond the veil.

When you look at me
There is complete restoration
When you look at me
There is also reconciliation.

When you look at me
I was never a mistake
When you look at me
I was never a phony or fake.

When you look at me
I am nothing but holiness
When you look at me
I am nothing but righteousness.

When you look at me
You see nothing but the blood on Jesus
When you at me
Freedom is a guarantee, a must.

Walking Down the Aisle with the One She Chose

Walking down the aisle with the one she chose
She has always known him
Before the foundations of the world, she supposed.

She chose him
To dwell in her courts
None would compare
Others always came up short.

There was a difference
In the man she chose
God must have approved
And that's what mattered the most.

By faith she opened her heart
Up to this only man
She was willing to take a risk
It was worth it to take a stand.

FROM BROKEN PIECES TO PEACE

The Lord used this man
To open her heart
Her love was locked away
It was difficult from the start.

Not only by knowing him
Was she able to finally love herself
It was painful for her
Her love for God and him caused
all negativity to melt.

By her faith in God
Was the only way this could be done
Many nights of crying, fasting, and praying
Was this mountain conquered and won.

It was God's intent all along
For this man and woman to be together
He made them one
To go through any stormy weather.

Walking down the aisle
With the one she chose
Before this moment
It wasn't easy as you suppose.

Nothing worth having
Isn't easy, you have to fight
It was well worth it
It was accomplished by His spirit and not by might
She chose to believe
Although there were times that were rough
She couldn't go by sight
Faith was a must.

Her prayer warriors stood by her and prayed
Fighting alongside her to help her through
She didn't and wouldn't give up
For the outcome depending on the Lord she knew.

Walking down the aisle
To meet her chosen mate
She is finally so pleased
Her time had come, she no longer had to wait.

Bearing It All

Bearing it all
For the sake of freedom
Loosing the bands
For all not just some.

If my telling my grief and pain
Sets you free
It was worth it all
Charge it to a heavenly deed.

To see the light in your eyes again
The pep in your step
No longer in sorrow
The joy you accept.

If your darkness is traded
In for the day
The fee I was charged
Was worth the price I had to pay.

Bearing it all
For the sake of the masses
Heart completely exposed
I refused to be passive.

If my testimony
Rescues you
It proves
The Word is true.

If bearing it all
Sets you free
Thank you, Father,
For using me.

Look Within

Look within
That's where your freedom will be found
It's there you'll find
The real true sound.

Believe in yourself
When no one else will
Be your own best fan
It'll be more real.

Looking outside first
To others is much confusion
They're winging life too
Is my only conclusion.

Their perspective at times
Is only fitting for them
Your trials they didn't face
Their misunderstanding makes your light more dim.

Trust in yourself more
A lot was invested you
Higher standards
Should be your only view.

Look within
What you know came from your maker
What you have
Didn't come from the fakers.

It's a hard to swallow
Many don't have your best interest at heart
The sooner you learn it
Being defeated will soon part.

It's the truth
If you'll believe what I'm saying
Stop casting your pearls
Before those that's faking.

Look within
To find strength might wisdom and power
Trust your first mind
It'll get you through your darkest hour.

Look within
There's plenty of grace mercy and love
Trust *you*
It's get you through what tough.

FROM BROKEN PIECES TO PEACE

People will tell you
What's really only suitable for them
Trust they don't qualify
Their non-prosperous life should be the hint.

Look within
Trust what *you* know
Just hush and be still
The knowledge and wisdom will flow.

Every answer you'll find
Was there all along
It's much more peaceful
To dance to your own song.

I know,
I finally looked within
The moment I did
It was then and only then I started to win.

Chapter 10

Getting out of Relationship Ruts and Staying out

The best thing I'd say is *prevention, prevention, prevention*. The Bible, the Living Word is a sure book of wisdom for every relationship problem or prevention of relationship problems if not ignored.

Proverbs 1 NASB

> ¹The proverbs of Solomon the son of David, king of Israel: ²To know wisdom and instruction, to discern the sayings of understanding, ³To receive instruction in wise behavior, righteousness, justice, and equity; ⁴To give prudence to the [a]naive, To the

youth knowledge and discretion, [5]A wise man will hear and increase in learning, And a man of understanding will acquire wise counsel, [6]To understand a proverb and a figure, the words of the wise and their riddles. [7]The fear of the Lord is the beginning of knowledge; fools despise wisdom and instruction. The Enticement of Sinners [8]Hear, my son, your father's instruction And do not forsake your mother's teaching; [9]Indeed, they are a graceful wreath to your head And [b]ornaments about your neck. [10]My son, if sinners entice you, Do not consent. [11]If they say, "Come with us, Let us lie in wait for blood, Let us ambush the innocent without cause; [12]Let us swallow them alive like Sheol, Even whole, as those who go down to the pit; [13]We will find all kinds of precious wealth, We will fill our houses with spoil; [14]Throw in your lot [c]with us, We shall all have one purse," [15]My son, do not walk in the way with them. Keep your feet from their path, [16]For their feet run to evil And they hasten to shed blood.

[17]Indeed, it is [d]useless to spread the baited net in the sight of any [e]bird; [18]But they lie in wait for their own blood; They ambush their own lives. [19]So are the ways of everyone who gains by violence; It takes away the life of its possessors.

Wisdom Warns

[20]Wisdom shouts in the street, She [f]lifts her voice in the square; [21]At the head of the noisy streets she cries out; At the entrance of the gates in the city she utters her sayings: [22]"How long, O [g]naive ones, will you love [h]being simple-minded? And scoffers delight themselves in scoffing And fools hate knowledge? [23]"Turn to my reproof, Behold, I will pour out my spirit on you; I will make my words known to you. [24]"Because I called and you refused, I stretched out my hand and no one paid attention; [25]And you neglected all my counsel And did not want my reproof; [26]I will also laugh at your calamity; I will mock when your dread comes, [27]When your dread comes like a storm And your calamity comes like a whirlwind, When distress and anguish come

upon you. [28]"Then they will call on me, but I will not answer; They will seek me diligently but they will not find me, [29]Because they hated knowledge And did not choose the fear of the Lord. [30] "They would not accept my counsel, They spurned all my reproof. [31]"So they shall eat of the fruit of their own way And be satiated with their own devices. [32]"For the waywardness of the [i]naive will kill them, And the complacency of fools will destroy them. [33]"But he who listens to me shall [j]live securely And will be at ease from the dread of evil."

Proverbs 2 NASB

[1]My son, if you will receive my words And treasure my commandments within you, [2]Make your ear attentive to wisdom, Incline your heart to understanding; [3]For if you cry for discernment, [a]Lift your voice for understanding; [4]If you seek her as silver And search for her as for hidden treasures; [5]Then you will discern the fear of the Lord And discover the knowledge of

God. [6]For the Lord gives wisdom; From His mouth come knowledge and understanding. [7]He stores up sound wisdom for the upright; He is a shield to those who walk in integrity, [8]Guarding the paths of justice, And He preserves the way of His godly ones. [9]Then you will discern righteousness and justice And equity and every good course. [10]For wisdom will enter your heart And knowledge will be pleasant to your soul; [11]Discretion will guard you, Understanding will watch over you, [12]To deliver you from the way of evil, from the man who speaks perverse things; [13]From those who leave the paths of uprightness to walk in the ways of darkness; [14]Who delight in doing evil And rejoice in the perversity of evil; [15]Whose paths are crooked, And who are devious in their ways;

[16]To deliver you from the strange woman,

From the [b]adulteress who flatters with her words; [17]That leaves the companion of her youth And forgets the covenant of her God;

[18]For her house [c]sinks down to death And her racks lead to the [d]dead; [19]None who go to her return again, Nor do they reach the paths of life.

[20]So you will walk in the way of good men

And keep to the paths of the righteous. [21]For the upright will [e]live in the land And the blameless will remain in it; [22]But the wicked will be cut off from the land And the treacherous will be uprooted from it.

Psalm 51 KJV

> Have mercy upon me, O God, according to thy lovingkindness: according unto the multitude of thy tender mercies blot out my transgressions.
>
> [2]Wash me thoroughly from mine iniquity, and cleanse me from my sin.
>
> [3]For I acknowledge my transgressions: and my sin is ever before me.

⁴Against thee, thee only, have I sinned, and done this evil in thy sight: that thou mightest be justified when thou speakest, and be clear when thou judgest.

⁵Behold, I was shapen in iniquity; and in sin did my mother conceive me.

⁶Behold, thou desirest truth in the inward parts: and in the hidden part thou shalt make me to know wisdom.

⁷Purge me with hyssop, and I shall be clean: wash me, and I shall be whiter than snow.

⁸Make me to hear joy and gladness; that the bones which thou hast broken may rejoice.

⁹Hide thy face from my sins, and blot out all mine iniquities.

¹⁰Create in me a clean heart, O God; and renew a right spirit within me.

¹¹Cast me not away from thy presence; and take not thy holy spirit from me.

¹²Restore unto me the joy of thy salvation; and uphold me with thy free spirit.

¹³Then will I teach transgressors thy ways; and sinners shall be converted unto thee.

¹⁴Deliver me from bloodguiltiness, O God, thou God of my salvation: and my tongue shall sing aloud of thy righteousness.

¹⁵O Lord, open thou my lips; and my mouth shall shew forth thy praise.

¹⁶For thou desirest not sacrifice; else would I give it: thou delightest not in burnt offering.

¹⁷The sacrifices of God are a broken spirit: a broken and a contrite heart, O God, thou wilt not despise.

¹⁸Do good in thy good pleasure unto Zion: build thou the walls of Jerusalem.

¹⁹Then shalt thou be pleased with the sacrifices of righteousness, with burnt offering and whole

burnt offering: then shall they offer bullocks upon thine altar.

Psalm 51 KJV

Have mercy upon me, O God, according to thy lovingkindness: according unto the multitude of thy tender mercies blot out my transgressions.

2 Wash me throughly from mine iniquity, and cleanse me from my sin.

3 For I acknowledge my transgressions: and my sin is ever before me.

4 Against thee, thee only, have I sinned, and done this evil in thy sight: that thou mightest be justified when thou speakest, and be clear when thou judgest.

5 Behold, I was shapen in iniquity; and in sin did my mother conceive me.

6 Behold, thou desirest truth in the inward parts: and in the hidden part thou shalt make me to know wisdom.

7 Purge me with hyssop, and I shall be clean: wash me, and I shall be whiter than snow.

8 Make me to hear joy and gladness; that the bones which thou hast broken may rejoice.

9 Hide thy face from my sins, and blot out all mine iniquities.

10 Create in me a clean heart, O God; and renew a right spirit within me.

11 Cast me not away from thy presence; and take not thy holy spirit from me.

12 Restore unto me the joy of thy salvation; and uphold me with thy free spirit.

13 Then will I teach transgressors thy ways; and sinners shall be converted unto thee.

14 Deliver me from bloodguiltiness, O God, thou God of my salvation: and my tongue shall sing aloud of thy righteousness.

15 O Lord, open thou my lips; and my mouth shall shew forth thy praise.

16 For thou desirest not sacrifice; else would I give it: thou delightest not in burnt offering.

17 The sacrifices of God are a broken spirit: a broken and a contrite heart, O God, thou wilt not despise.

18 Do good in thy good pleasure unto Zion: build thou the walls of Jerusalem.

19 Then shalt thou be pleased with the sacrifices of righteousness, with burnt offering and whole burnt offering: then shall they offer bullocks upon thine altar.

Psalm 121

1 I will lift up mine eyes unto the hills, from whence cometh my help.

2 My help cometh from the Lord, which made heaven and earth.

> ³He will not suffer thy foot to be moved: he that keepeth thee will not slumber.
>
> ⁴Behold, he that keepeth Israel shall neither slumber nor sleep.
>
> ⁵The Lord is thy keeper: the Lord is thy shade upon thy right hand.
>
> ⁶The sun shall not smite thee by day, nor the moon by night.
>
> ⁷The Lord shall preserve thee from all evil: he shall preserve thy soul.
>
> ⁸The Lord shall preserve thy going out and thy coming in from this time forth, and even for evermore.

John 1:1–5 KJV

> ¹In the beginning was the Word, and the Word was with God, and the Word was God.
>
> ²The same was in the beginning with God.
>
> ³All things were made by him; and without him was not any thing made that was made.

⁴In him was life; and the life was the light of men.

⁵And the light shineth in darkness; and the darkness comprehended it not.

1 John 1:6-10

6 If we say that we have fellowship with him, and walk in darkness, we lie, and do not the truth:

7 But if we walk in the light, as he is in the light, we have fellowship one with another, and the blood of Jesus Christ his Son cleanseth us from all sin.

8 If we say that we have no sin, we deceive ourselves, and the truth is not in us.

9 If we confess our sins, he is faithful and just to forgive us our sins, and to cleanse us from all unrighteousness.

10 If we say that we have not sinned, we make him a liar, and his word is not in us.

1 Corinthians 13, The Message

> [1] If I speak with human eloquence and angelic ecstasy but don't love, I'm nothing but the creaking of a rusty gate.
>
> [2] If I speak God's Word with power, revealing all his mysteries and making everything plain as day, and if I have faith that says to a mountain, "Jump," and it jumps, but I don't love, I'm nothing.
>
> [3-7] If I give everything I own to the poor and even go to the stake to be burned as a martyr, but I don't love, I've gotten nowhere. So, no matter what I say, what I believe, and what I do, I'm bankrupt without love.
>
> Love never gives up.
>
> Love cares more for others than for self.
>
> Love doesn't want what it doesn't have.
>
> Love doesn't strut,
>
> Doesn't have a swelled head,

Doesn't force itself on others,

Isn't always "me first,"

Doesn't fly off the handle,

Doesn't keep score of the sins of others,

Doesn't revel when others grovel,

Takes pleasure in the flowering of truth,

Puts up with anything,

Trusts God always,

Always looks for the best,

Never looks back,

But keeps going to the end.

8-10 Love never dies. Inspired speech will be over some day; praying in tongues will end; understanding will reach its limit. We know only a portion of the truth, and what we say about God is always incomplete. But when the Complete arrives, our incompletes will be canceled.

11 When I was an infant at my mother's breast, I gurgled and

> cooed like any infant. When I grew up, I left those infant ways for good.
>
> ¹²We don't yet see things clearly. We're squinting in a fog, peering through a mist. But it won't be long before the weather clears and the sun shines bright! We'll see it all then, see it all as clearly as God sees us, knowing him directly just as he knows us!
>
> ¹³But for right now, until that completeness, we have three things to do to lead us toward that consummation: Trust steadily in God, hope unswervingly, love extravagantly. And the best of the three is love.

James 1:19–27, The Message

> ¹⁹⁻²¹Post this at all the intersections, dear friends: Lead with your ears, follow up with your tongue, and let anger straggle along in the rear. God's righteousness doesn't grow from human anger. So throw all spoiled virtue and cancerous evil in the garbage. In simple humility, let our gardener, God, land-

scape you with the Word, making a salvation-garden of your life.

²²⁻²⁴Don't fool yourself into thinking that you are a listener when you are anything but, letting the Word go in one ear and out the other. Act on what you hear! Those who hear and don't act are like those who glance in the mirror, walk away, and two minutes later have no idea who they are, what they look like.

²⁵But whoever catches a glimpse of the revealed counsel of God—the free life!—even out of the corner of his eye, and sticks with it, is no distracted scatterbrain but a man or woman of action. That person will find delight and affirmation in the action.

²⁶⁻²⁷Anyone who sets himself up as "religious" by talking a good game is self-deceived. This kind of religion is hot air and only hot air. Real religion, the kind that passes muster before God the Father, is this: Reach out to the homeless and loveless in their plight, and guard against corruption from the godless world.

Chapter 11

Advice from My Dear Mom and Grandmother

I'm sure anyone's mother and grandmother can give them good advice. I think this is one of the treasures and moments I will forever share with my mom and grandmother. Our long talks about life. Many days I wish I would've listened. I'm sure most of us can say the same. Our parents and grandparents don't tell us things to keep us from living and having fun, but they were there before us. They've been there and done that. All they ever want us not to do is make the same mistakes as them. But most of us want to be adults too early by making our own decisions. But hind sight, it sure does pay to listen. And I try my best to hand down what I've learned to my own child. I'm sure you've heard some of the following advice:

When you're in a good relationship, keep folk out of your business.

Keep folk out of your home. Don't borrow sugar from them because they'll have a reason to come back and borrow it from you.

Everyone is not your friend. Be careful who you take advice from.

Be a friend to your own self. Be comfortable in your own skin.

Watch your friends, not your enemies. You *know* your enemies don't like you.

A miserable person loves company. Don't you be the one they keep company with.

Don't nobody love you but me and your grandmomma.

A leopard never loses its spots.

Don't mistreat people. What goes around, comes around.

You're pretty, but a man only wants one thing.

A hard head makes a soft behind.

You make your bed hard, you gon' lie in it.

Anything worth having ain't gonna come easy.

I'm your momma, I'm the only real friend you have.

Folk ain't loving you all like they say.

Everybody that say they saved . . . ain't saved for real.

Let a man be a man. Don't feel sorry for them (the older I get, the better I understand this one).

Chapter 12

YOU ARE NOT BROKEN: MY CONCLUSION

It took me forty-six years of trial and error to realize *I am not broken*. I've just dealt with many broken men. I refuse to believe anything else. Male or female, it's time we stop taking things and life so personal. We all come from different backgrounds. Some of us come from not the best of circumstance. But there are those who continue to use their "not so good" upbringing as an excuse to stay broken rather than face their personal issues and grow up. *You* refuse to take what life hands you through these broken individuals. Only accept what's necessary in your life. If that woman/man for some reason does not want to accept you for who you are—a king or queen—that's on them. You are the star of your own show and don't let someone who obviously don't know what good looks like take it away from *you* Many women and men refuse to be whole and are only attracted to broken people—you guessed it—like them. Weak *cannot* deal with strong. Men and women, stop trying to fix a broken individual. It's just not your responsibility. It's their responsibility to become a whole strong person. I am so thankful I understand this now. Don't feel sorry for them and for yourself! Pick yourself up and be the king and queens you are! That special someone who's especially tailored for you is on the way. And never doubt that for a moment. I've never been married, but I refuse to settle! Forget that! I finally know and come to grips with the worth of Kimi Yashiko! And trust she deserves the best! So do you! In the end, those who refuse to accept you and love you for who you are *will regret it* Just keep it moving!

Also by Kimi Bivins

In this compilation of memoir, poetry, and reflections, Bivins addresses important issues of the church with emotional depth while at the same time providing insight into what it's like raising a child on one's own. *Overcoming a Broken Heart* considers the importance of worship, the impact of relationships, the role of an active father in a child's life, the goal of working toward God's purpose in our life, and the responsibility of the church to aid in forgiveness.

About the Author

Kimi Bivins is a twenty-six-year army veteran, born in Newark, New Jersey but raised in Southeastern Alabama. She works for the postal service. She's currently in school receiving her second degree in Human Resource Management. She has a daughter, Angel. Kimi loves poetry and songwriting. "From Broken Pieces to Peace" is her second book after her debut book "Overcoming a Broken Heart" in 2012.

www.ingramcontent.com/pod-product-compliance
Lightning Source LLC
Chambersburg PA
CBHW022009120526
44592CB00034B/762

9781951490614